OLD BRIDGE PUBLIC LIBRARY

The Pennsylvania Dutch

BOOKS BY EVA DEUTSCH COSTABEL
A New England Village
The Pennsylvania Dutch: Craftsmen and Farmers

The Pennsylvania Dutch

CRAFTSMEN AND FARMERS

written and illustrated by EVA DEUTSCH COSTABEL

Atheneum   1986   New York

869303

Many thanks to
John Ward Willson Loose, President of the Lancaster Historical Society,
for taking time to check the manuscript and artwork
and for his valuable advice.

Copyright © 1986 by Eva Deutsch Costabel
All rights reserved. No part of this book may be reproduced
or transmitted in any form or by any means, electronic or
mechanical, including photocopying, recording, or by any
information storage and retrieval system, without
permission in writing from the publisher.

Atheneum
Macmillan Publishing Company
866 Third Avenue, New York, NY 10022

Composition by P & M Typesetting, Inc., Waterbury, Connecticut
Printed and bound by South China Printing Company, Hong Kong

Typography by Mary Ahern

10 9 8 7 6 5 4 3 2 1

Library of Congress Cataloging-in-Publication Data

Costabel, Eva Deutsch.   The Pennsylvania Dutch.

SUMMARY: Describes the crafts of Pennsylvania
Dutch living in a rural atmosphere. Includes making
quilts, pottery, and tin and tole ware.
1. Pennsylvania Dutch—Social life and customs—
Juvenile literature. 2. Handicraft—Pennsylvania—
Juvenile literature.   3. Pennsylvania—Social life and
customs—Juvenile literature. [1. Pennsylvania Dutch—
Social life and customs. 2. Handicraft—Pennsylvania]
I. Title.
F160.G3C67   1986   974.8'00431   86-3334
ISBN 0-689-31281-4

J
974.8
cos
c.1

TO NEW YORK CITY, U.S.A., AND ITS PEOPLE.

On June 10, 1949, I sailed into New York harbor with my sister Erika. I was penniless. She had one hundred dollars which she shared with me. A young woman broken in mind, spirit, and body, having witnessed and survived the horrors of the Holocaust, here I was able to rebuild my shattered life. Along the way, I met many people, who with their compassion, faith in me, good intent, and plain humanity helped me to become whole once again. Without these kind people, who opened the doors for me so that I could become an author, painter, designer, and teacher, I could never have lifted my head from darkness into light.

Contents

Introduction

The Pennsylvania Dutch have made important contributions to the history of our country. More correctly, these groups should be called the Pennsylvania Germans. The English, who settled first, mispronounced the word "deutsch," meaning German. They called the new, mainly German, settlers "Dutch" and the name stuck.

In the seventeenth century, central Europe was in great turmoil. Ambitious rulers were fighting wars for political and religious dominance, and the population suffered. Families were wiped out. Many became homeless, losing all their possessions. They had little hope for a better tomorrow.

At this time, William Penn, an English Quaker with liberal ideas, was traveling the Rhine region of Germany, trying to enlist people to settle in Pennsylvania. In 1683, the first German-speaking settlers arrived in the New World.

Many of them came from the Palatinate region of Germany, the region along the Rhine river. Others came from the lower Rhine area—Alsace-Lorraine, Switzerland, Silesia, Saxony, Moravia—and even the Scandinavian countries.

The journey was full of danger, but the immigrants brought with them great hope for a better future, faith in God, and a willingness to work long and hard.

The Quakers were the first religious group to arrive. They were then followed by many others, including the Mennonites, Moravians, and Amish. In the early years, the members of all these various religious groups learned how to live and work together.

The Pennsylvania Germans came from many different levels of society. Some were university graduates. Others were highly skilled craftsmen: carpenters, weavers, glass blowers, engravers, blacksmiths, and potters. They were a desirable group of immigrants coming to develop a new land. Many of the skilled craftsmen settled near Philadelphia, in an area which came to be known as Germantown.

The majority of the German settlers, though, were farmers, and they were happy to settle on the rich soil of Pennsylvania, mainly in the counties of Berks, Lehigh, Lebanon, York, Dauphin, and Lancaster.

The German farmers worked hard to build homes, plant vegetable gardens, raise fruit trees in their orchards, and grow the wheat for their bread. They developed progressive farming methods and were soon producing more than they needed for their own needs. They sold the excess to their neighbors and the farmland soon had the reputation as the breadbasket of America.

The Pennsylvania Germans are known for their hard work, their language, crafts, and above all, their love for family, community, and church.

Family and Home

The Pennsylvania Germans had a strong feeling for family life. The farmer needed a large work force, so many children were considered a blessing. An average family might include ten children. Older members of the family—parents and grandparents—also lived with the young people. A separate addition to the house might be built for them.

The undisputed head of the family was the father and he took care of all financial matters and the education of his sons. Besides basic farming skills, the early settlers also had to supply many of the crafts needed for a well-run farm. Sons often worked as apprentices to their fathers.

While the farmers worked in the fields, their sons brought them food and water. The boys also cared for the chickens and other fowl, while the care of the cattle and other farm animals was the father's job.

The girls were trained by their mothers to milk the cows, churn butter, make and mend everybody's clothing, tend the fruit and vegetable gardens, cook, bake, and keep the house clean. Skill in these housewifely arts was regarded as something to be proud of and future suitors saw this as an important asset when choosing a wife.

The Pennsylvania Germans took good care of all their possessions. The houses and barns were swept clean. Floors were scrubbed, furniture was polished, and cutlery was kept shining.

The Kitchen

The fireplace was used both for cooking and for heating the kitchen, and this is where the family spent most of their time.

Many household chores were done at a large worktable, called a sawbuck table. China dishes and cups were stored in a decorated, glass-doored cupboard, called a Dutch cupboard. At the front of the shelf, spoons might be displayed.

In one corner of the kitchen there might be a hanging cupboard with a decorative piece of pottery on the shelf. Under this, the family Bible would be stored in a section closed off by a door.

Carved boxes for holding salt and cutlery hung on the wall. There could also be a copper warming pan, perhaps decorated with birds. In another corner might also be a grandfather clock or a prominent armchair which was to be used by the father.

Framed birth and baptismal certificates might also decorate the walls.

The Bedchamber

The bedchamber floors were mostly bare and the room was clean and uncluttered. There might be a wooden cradle for a baby. Clothing was stored in a wooden wardrobe, a wooden chest held linens, and other articles were stored in a chest of drawers. There might also be a wooden chair with a heart-shaped cutout on its back.

The four-poster bed dominated the bedchamber. The mattress was filled with corn husks or straw and rested on the rope-laced bedframe. It was covered with white homespun linen. On top of this were one or more comforters made of feathers stuffed in a white-and-blue checked case, or a case made of wool. The pillows were also feather-filled. The top cover was a heavy woven coverlet or a colorful quilt. The bedsheet and linens were often embroidered in fine cross-stitching with the owner's name.

Linen and Wool

It didn't take long before the Pennsylvania Dutch settlers planted their first crop of flax, from which they could make linen cloth.

The harvested flax first had to be cleaned of its woody impurities. This very tedious task was one of the chores of the mother and daughters. The clean flax was then spun into thread on the spinning wheel.

Often, the spinning became a social outlet for the farm women. By getting together to do the work, they could exchange news from the village and gossip a bit as they worked.

The settlers also needed wool clothing to protect themselves from the cold winters in Pennsylvania. After clearing the countryside of predatory animals such as wolves, bears, and panthers, they started to raise sheep for wool.

The month of May was the time for sheep shearing—another great social event. The sheep were washed by being driven into a stream. Then they were sheared and the wool was spread on the grass to dry in the sun.

The production of wool was small at first, so the settlers invented cloth of a mixture of linen and wool called linsey-woolsey. When town women traveled the Pennsylvania countryside, they ridiculed the German women for their clothing made of this coarse homespun, but for the hard-working farm women, it was the proper attire.

The English saw this wool production cutting into profits of the English wool merchants, but the settlers continued raising sheep, and in time developed a strong weaving industry.

Weaving

Although most of the spinning was done at home, usually only a small amount of the weaving could be done there. Most families had a small handloom to weave cloth for everyday use.

The rest of the work was given to a professional weaver, who made the yarn into linen, wool, and linsey-woolsey. Linen or linsey-woolsey was used for household linens and many articles of clothing. The more unpurified kind of linen was used to make the Conestoga wagon covers. Pure wool cloth was used mainly for the family's best Sunday clothes.

Another important product of the loom was the double-woven woolen coverlet, a type of work for which the Pennsylvania Dutch are known. The typical design on this might be a pine tree or a snowflake woven in the traditional colors of white and blue.

As the Pennsylvania Dutch colony became more established, the desire for more elaborate designs also grew. Weavers traveled the countryside with sample books of complex and colorful designs.

Many of the patterns were of a patriotic nature, but trees, birds, and flowers were also used quite often. Some coverlets had the owner's name or the name of the weaver woven into the fabric, along with the date and place of weaving.

The colors used were mainly blue, white, brown, and yellow, until the beginning of the nineteenth century, when the Jacquard loom was invented and brought to America. This loom could produce more complicated patterns in more varied colors. Fine pieces of weaving were precious possessions of the home.

Quilting

The Pennsylvania Dutch woman found her true expression in the creation of quilts.

Creating colorful patchwork design squares was a way to use every scrap of valuable fabric, even after the clothing or linens made from it were worn. It was also a welcome social outlet for the hardworking farm women. At a quilting bee, women got together to exchange news and a bit of gossip as they sewed the layers of the quilt with designs of fancy stitches.

A young girl made quilts as part of her dowry and stored them in the dower chest until her marriage. A friendship quilt was made for the bride. Her friends cut out the pieces and she sewed them together into a quilt. Women would trade squares with one another for greater variety.

The star was a popular motif, as were baskets of flowers, fruit, eagles, birds, and acorns. Some designs had poetic names like Star of Bethlehem, Rising Star, Path Through the Woods, Lone Star, Tumbling Block, Cherry Spray, Barn Raising, and Autumn Leaf.

Barns

One of the most impressive sights on a Pennsylvania German farm was the barn. At first, barns were nothing more than huge "log cabins," but as the farmers became more settled, they built their barns of stone. These buildings were usually the largest on the farm—even bigger than the farmhouse!

The hayloft was on the second floor of the barn. If it was possible, the barn was built against a hill so that wagons could go directly into the loft to unload hay. When there was no hill, a ramp would be built for the same purpose.

The animals were housed on the barn's first floor. The roof on the side of the barn above their stalls had a large overhang. This gave the farmer protection from bad weather.

The Pennsylvania German barns were known for the brightly colored geometric designs painted on them. In Europe, these hex signs were believed to keep evil spirits away. The Pennsylvania Germans probably used the designs more for their decorative value than for any other reason. No matter what the reason, the hex symbols are what come to mind when we think of the Pennsylvania Dutch.

Scissor Cutting

The Pennsylvania Germans had a number of different ways to turn paper into decorations for their homes. One of these was scissor cutting. Shapes were cut out of the paper and the paper was then used in many places in the house.

Shelf paper, sometimes made from cut-out newspaper, decorated the pantry shelves. From time to time, it would be replaced with fresh pieces.

Paper was also used to decorate the mantel. This was usually made of cut-out white tissue paper laid over a dark blue background. Hearts, birds, and scalloped edges were often used in these designs.

Cut paper doilies made from orange tissue paper were also very popular. They were placed all over the house—under candles, small dishes, and fancy cakes baked for festivities.

The Pennsylvania Germans combined scissor cutting with fractur to create beautiful illuminated works commemorating important events in their lives.

In birth and baptismal certificates (*taufscheine*), the paper was delicately cut out and the name and year of birth, along with blessings for the life of the newborn, would be written in fine calligraphy. Marriage certificates were decorated in a similar manner, and so were *haus-segen* or "house-blessings," which asked blessings for the family and the farm.

This type of artwork is also seen in the *liebesbrief,* or love letters. These are much like our Valentines and, in fact, were sent on Valentine's Day. However, they were also sent all year round to the loved one as an expression of affection. These cards would often be round in shape and would have cut-out designs and messages painted in bright colors.

Children also loved this form of art and some of the brightest and most imaginative examples come from them. Besides creating pieces for their own enjoyment, some of their work was used as decorations at Christmas and Easter.

Pennsylvania Dutch Folk Art

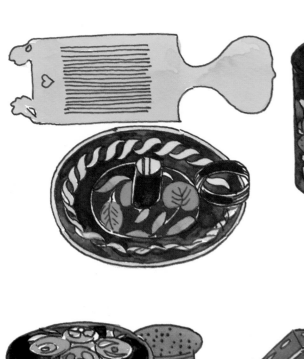

Tinware

After the settlers had taken care of all of their most important needs, they began to think about decorating their homes with the designs they remembered from their homeland. Thus developed the art of decorated tinware. The plain tinware was first imported from England, but later was crafted by the Pennsylvania Germans themselves.

This ware was not made of solid tin. Tin had to come from England and was scarce in the new land, so the utensils were made of thin sheets of iron that were dipped into molten tin to keep the iron from rusting. This tin coating also made it easier to solder. Tin is lighter and easier to care for than iron, and housewives readily accepted this innovation.

In the early years, most tinware was painted freehand, but later on a stenciling technique was used. We find these painted designs mostly on coffee and tea caddies, trinket boxes, tea kettles, trays, and cream pitchers. Flowers were painted most often, but there were also designs of birds and fruit.

Some tin was punched rather than painted. This technique was used mainly for lanterns and footwarmers. The perforations created interesting designs when the light shone through. Holes in the footwarmers let out the heat so that people could keep warm on cold winter days. Punched tin was also used for the doors of "pie safes"—large cupboards for storing baked goods. The holes allowed air to flow over the pies and keep them from getting moldy.

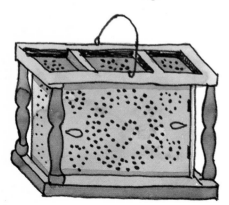

Pottery

Pottery was an important craft in America because most settlers could not bring crockery with them when they immigrated. The American potteries produced everyday objects for the housewife's use. At first, the pieces were crude, without glaze or decoration, but by 1750, potters had begun to experiment with different types of glazes.

The most popular pottery of the Pennsylvania Dutch was redware. Its name comes from the reddish color of the local clay. Redware is easy to produce as it needs a relatively low temperature for firing. Generally, it was decorated with a type of design, called *sgraffito,* which was scratched into the glazed coating so that the original clay under it showed through.

Designs on pottery included birds, flowers, horsemen, and human figures. German sayings, often humorous, were also used as decoration.

Decorated pieces were fairly rare and used mostly as showpieces. Most objects of the Pennsylvania Dutch were for daily use and had little or no decoration.

Some Pennsylvania German houses had tiled roofs, similar to the ones on their homes in Germany. Roof tiles with ridges so that the rainwater could run off easily were also made by the potter.

The potter's craft was a self-sufficient one. He could operate using local resources. Clay was dug from the riverbanks. Local stone was used to build the kiln. Firewood was cut from local forests. Pottery was, for the most part, a family industry and sons learned the craft from their fathers.

Stiegel Glass

The finest glass of the eighteenth century in the New World was named after Henry William Stiegel, who was born in Cologne, Germany, in 1729. In Manheim, Pennsylvania, where he settled, his friends affectionately called him "Baron."

Stiegel first arrived in Philadelphia in 1750 and he began work at an iron-casting furnace he named "Elizabeth" after his wife. Later, he used this same furnace to start his glassworks.

Although not a craftsman himself, he hired and directed highly skilled European craftsmen. Many of them were newly arrived from Europe. Together they produced what came to be regarded as the finest glass in the New World.

The Stiegel shop produced a wide variety of glass pieces: bottles, pitchers, mugs, jugs, vases, glasses, flasks, bowls, and candlestick holders. Later, it produced window glass and glass for chemical use.

Stiegel glass was finely colored, etched, engraved, pressed, and enamaled. The handpainted brightly colored glass pieces, decorated with birds and animals of all sorts, were well known and liked.

Best known were his transparent and white flint or crystal glass. Other glass pieces were in green, amber, blue, and amethyst.

Stiegel became a wealthy and prominent citizen. At first, he had ten people working for him, but the number grew steadily as the demand for his glass increased. At one point, he was able to employ one hundred and thirty workers.

Woodenware

In their spare time, gifted Pennsylvania Dutch people carved special wooden objects that were mostly for kitchen use. These included springerle molds, marzipan molds, and butter and maple sugar molds.

A springerle mold was a flat wooden board with designs carved into hard wood, like maple, oak, and walnut, which would resist the oven's heat. The designs had great variety and included such subjects as farm animals, houses, people, birds, and wild animals. The board came in different sizes and had as many as twenty-four designs. When the dough was pressed into the mold and baked, the shapes stood out in relief, on the cookies.

Besides those flat cookie forms, there were also wooden cylinders with carved figures, which were used like rolling pins. They also imprinted their designs into the dough.

The marzipan mold was used mostly around holidays and these small molds were used to make almond candy in the shape of flowers, birds, and animals. Maple sugar candy forms had simple designs such as maple leaves, birds, and animals.

The most commonly carved kitchen item was the butter mold. About two hundred different designs were created for these molds. The most common of these designs are the five pointed star, sheaf of wheat, and various birds.

There are so many different designs for butter prints because they served to identify the family who produced the butter. This symbol is the predecessor of the modern trademark.

The most common mold was round-sided and the finished butter was put into a cylindrical wooden case, but other shapes were also made.

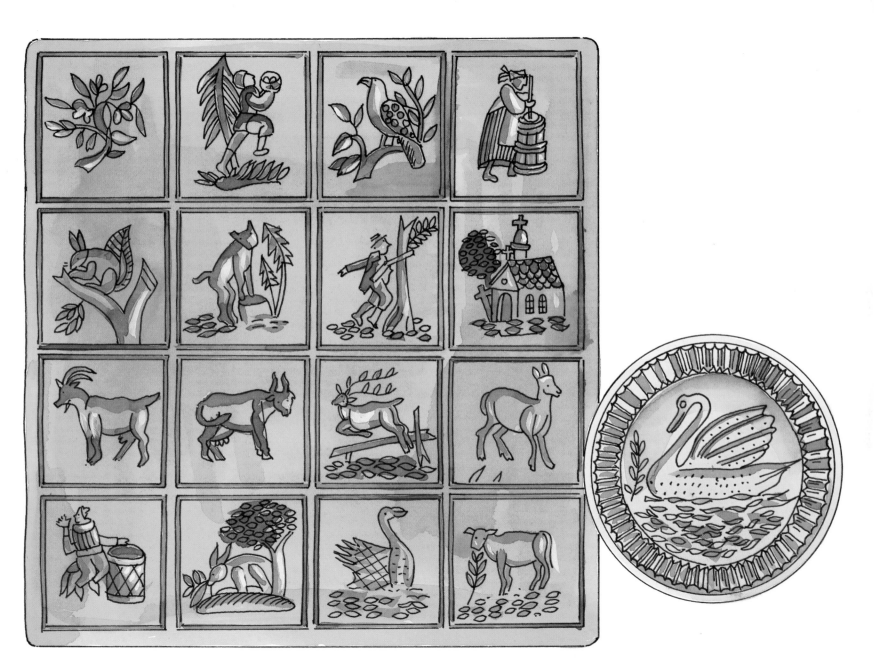

Decorated Woodenware

The Pennsylvania Dutch not only carved wood, they also painted it. Typical decorations can be seen on blanket chests, hat boxes, cradles, candle boxes, spice boxes, dough trays, and small pieces of furniture.

One type of painted wood ware, called Lehnware, was named for Joseph Lehn, a farmer who was born in 1798. He lived in Lititz, Pennsylvania, and lived to be ninety-four years old. He painted the small containers he made in bright and cheerful colors, usually in floral designs. His work was very popular, especially because he lived near a famous girls' school and the girls found that his tiny containers made lovely gifts. Many of Lehn's pieces were turned from sassafras wood.

Wilhelm Schimmel was a very famous American whittler who worked thirty years after the Civil War. He belonged to a group of wandering tramp craftsmen who would travel from village to village and whittle objects of art in exchange for a meal, lodging, drinks, or any other of his needs. He was most prolific and carved many small animals, but he was best known for his carved wooden eagles, which he painted in basic colors. One of his pieces is quite elaborate—an Adam and Eve composition called "Garden of Eden."

"Weberboxes," used for trinkets and various small objects, were made by an Amish bishop. His work was easily recognized by his use of the little red schoolhouse as a central theme.

Tombstone Art

The Pennsylvania Germans even embellished their tombstones with great care and skill.

Angels, the sun, moon, and stars were the usual subject matter of their designs, but the lily, the tree of life, and symbols from ancient times were also used. Occasionally, there might be a chiselled portrait of the departed.

Tombstones were mainly cut of redstone or slate. The inscriptions were usually in German.

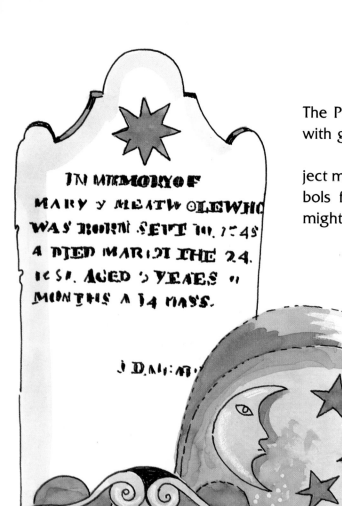

IN MEMORY OF
MARY J MEATWOLEWHC
WAS BORN SEPT 10, 1748
4 DIED MARCH THE 24.
1CS1. AGED 5 YEARS 11
MONTHS A 14 DAYS.

J D MEAT

Some tombstones were carved in hard wood, others were cast in iron, and still another type, quite rare, is the ceramic tombstone. Early potters created these for the members of their own families. They were made of light-colored clay and glazed and baked in kilns like any other piece of pottery. The glaze was usually gray, with cobalt blue inscriptions and simple designs.

Rarest of all were the ceramic tombstones in the shape of a lamb. These were made out of red clay and simply whitewashed.

Clocks

Clockmaking was a craft very much in demand by the Pennsylvania Dutch. Among the areas of Pennsylvania known for clockmaking were Lancaster, Reading, York, Kutztown, Coatesville, Lebanon, and New Holland. During the first half of the eighteenth century, a grandfather clock with inlaid hex signs and scrolls on the top of the hood was one of the area's most famous products.

Clockmakers like John Fisher of York and Jacob Gorgas of Ephrata made names for themselves in the trade and Martin Shreiner worked for forty years (from 1790 to 1830) and created more than three hundred and fifty clocks.

Before this, clocks were mostly imported from England and Holland, but some fine European clockmakers saw an opportunity to make a living in the New World and many of them came to America and settled in towns in Pennsylvania where there was a great demand for their skill.

The Blacksmith

Immigrant German blacksmiths brought their tools and knowledge to Pennsylvania and established iron foundries and blacksmith shops.

   The blacksmith in a rural community was a very necessary and busy man. He could make almost anything in iron the settlers needed. For the women's kitchens he made iron grates and pots and pans. Nails, tools, and carriage and wagon parts could be made for use by the farmer. The smith also made weather vanes, boot scrapers, wheel rims, sled runners, and many other objects for daily use.

   One of his most distinctive contributions were elaborately decorated wrought iron hardware. Door latches and hinges were worked into heart and tulip designs.

   The blacksmith put much of his creativity in these objects, so when he forged them, he also forged his place among the folk artists of the New World.

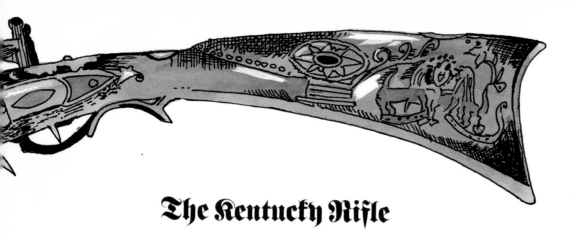

The Kentucky Rifle

This gun is considered one of the first guns of truly American design and was produced in the Conestoga Valley. Although it is called the Kentucky rifle, because it was used by many of the pioneers in Kentucky, it was designed and made by the Pennsylvania Germans in small shops during the 1700s.

The rifle weighed between seven and nine pounds and was fifty-five inches long. Its stock was made of curly maple or cherry or applewood. Many rifles were decorated with silver or brass in elaborate designs skillfully inlaid in the wood. Some Pennsylvania Germans believed that the designs were not only decorative, but that they gave the owner special powers.

The guns took a week to make and cost about twenty-five dollars each. If very elaborately decorated, a gun could cost as much as sixty dollars.

The rifle's design is believed to come from both the German snubnose rifle and the British musket. It combines the best qualities of each, being lighter and more accurate than either one.

During the Revolutionary War, the Pennsylvania rifles were called "Widowmakers" by the British.

The Conestoga Wagon

Another major contribution of the Pennsylvania Germans was the Conestoga wagon. Before the railroad, this was the main means of transportation for commerce. The name Conestoga comes from the Conestoga Creek over which the Indians carried furs to Philadelphia.

The wagon was pulled by a team of horses (usually six) able to travel the roughest roads. These horses, specially bred in the Conestoga Valley, were very large and could easily haul the 2000 to 3000 pounds of farm produce that the wagon carried to the town marketplace. Often, in the fall, more than a hundred wagons would travel on the old Lancaster pike to Philadelphia to sell produce and other farm products.

The wagon was built with great care and skill from hickory, oak, and poplar, and was reinforced with well-designed forged iron. The wheels were painted red and the bed, or body, was painted blue, with a sturdy linen cover for protection from rain, snow, sun, and wind.

The wagon also had a set of team bells of which the driver was very proud. It was a tradition that if the wagon driver needed help, he had to give up his bells to his rescuer. This is the origin of the saying, "Come home with your bells."

Bibliography

Davidson, Marshall B. *The American Heritage History of Colonial Antiques.* New York: American Heritage Publishing Co.

Hopf, Claudia and Don Palmquist. *Scherenschnitte.* Lebanon, PA: Applied Arts Publishers

Hornung, Clarence P. *The Treasury of American Design.* New York: Harry N. Abrams, Inc.

Hostetler, John A. *Amish Society.* Baltimore, MD: Johns Hopkins University Press

Kauffman, Henry J. *Pennsylvania Dutch: American Folk Art.* Mineola, NY: Dover Publications Inc.

Lichten, Frances. *Folk Art Motifs of Pennsylvania.* Mineola, NY: Dover Publications Inc.

———— *Folk Art of Rural Pennsylvania.* Mineola, NY: Dover Publications Inc.

Lipman, Jean. *American Folk Decoration.* Mineola, NY: Dover Publications Inc.

Lipman, Jean and Alice Winchester. *The Flowering of American Folk Art, 1776–1876.* New York: The Viking Press in cooperation with the Whitney Museum of American Art

Shea, John Gerald. *The Pennsylvania Dutch and Their Furniture.* New York: Van Nostrand Reinhold Co.

Smith, Elmer L. and Mel Horst. *Antiques of the Pennsylvania Dutch.* Lebanon, PA: Applied Arts Publishers

———— *Early Country Furniture.* Lebanon, PA: Applied Arts Publishers

———— *The Folk Art of Pennsylvania Dutchland.* Lebanon, PA: Applied Arts Publishers

———— *Tinware—Yesterday and Today.* Lebanon, PA: Applied Arts Publishers

Pennsylvania's Landmarks—From the Delaware to the Ohio. Lebanon, PA: Applied Arts Publishers

Index

A PARTIAL LISTING OF MUSEUMS
WITH AMERICAN FOLK ART COLLECTIONS

Abby Aldrich Rockefeller Folk Art Center, Williamsburg, VA
Brooklyn Museum, Decorative Arts Department, Brooklyn, NY
Hershey Estates Museum, Hershey, PA
Metropolitan Museum of Art, New York, NY
Museum of American Folk Art, New York, NY
New York Historical Society, New York, NY
Pennsylvania Farm Museum of Landis Valley, Pennsylvania
    Historical and Museum Commission, Lancaster, PA
Pennsylvania State Museum, Harrisburg, PA
Philadelphia Museum of Art, Philadelphia, PA
Smithsonian Institution, Washington, DC
The Whitney Museum of American Art, New York, NY
The Henry Francis du Pont Winterthur Museum, Winterthur, DE

Courtesy of Pennsylvania Farm Museum of Landis Valley,
    Pennsylvania Historical and Museum Commission, art on pages
    9, 10, 28, 30, 33, 38, 40

18th Century Pennsylvania German Farm Buildings Engraving
    Published 1757: A View of Bethlehem in Pennsylvania.
    Courtesy of the New York Historical Society, pg. 3.